MANNERS MATTER TO MAEVIS

Maevis MINDS HER MANNERS

Written by
Vicky Bureau
M.S., School Counseling

Illustrated by
Flavia Zuncheddu

A Starfish Book

SEAHORSE
PUBLISHING

Teaching Tips for Caregivers:

As a caregiver, you can help your child succeed in school by giving them a strong foundation in language and literacy skills and a desire to learn to read.

This book helps children grow by letting them practice reading skills.

Reading for pleasure and interest will help your child to develop reading skills and will give your child the opportunity to practice these skills in meaningful ways.

- Encourage your child to read on her own at home
- Encourage your child to practice reading aloud
- Encourage activities that require reading
- Establish a reading time
- Talk with your child
- Give your child writing materials

Teaching Tips for Teachers:

Research shows that one of the best ways for students to learn a new topic is to read about it.

Before Reading

- Read the "Words to Know" and discuss the meaning of each word.
- Read the back cover to see what the book is about.

During Reading

- When a student gets to a word that is unknown, ask them to look at the rest of the sentence to find clues to help with the meaning of the unknown word.
- Ask the student to write down any pages of the book that were confusing to them.

After Reading

- Discuss the main idea of the book.
- Ask students to give one detail that they learned in the book by showing a text dependent answer from the book.

TABLE OF CONTENTS

Meet Maevis

This is Maevis.

School **manners** matter to Maevis.

School manners are the rules and **expectations** for learning.

What Are Manners?

Manners are behaviors that show others kindness, respect, and **courtesy**.

Maevis uses her manners to be **mindful** of others.

Using Good Manners

Maevis sits with a friend
who is alone at lunch.

Maevis is kind.

Maevis says "please" and "thank you."

Maevis is **respectful**.

Maevis holds the door for her teacher.

Maevis is courteous.

Maevis raises her hand before speaking.

Maevis uses her manners in the classroom.

Maevis shares her pretzels at snack time.

Maevis uses her manners in
the cafeteria.

Maevis shares the ball.

Maevis uses her manners on the playground.

Maevis is mindful about how she makes others feel.

That's why Maevis minds her manners!

WORDS TO KNOW

courtesy (KUR-ti-see): good manners or politeness

expectations (ek-spek-TAY-shuhnz): the rules that tell us what is okay to do and not to do

manners (MAN-urs): the rules and expectations for learning; good behaviors

mindful (MINDE-fuhl): being careful and paying close attention

respectful (ri-SPEKT-fuhl): showing that you admire and pay attention to someone or something

INDEX

COMPREHENSION QUESTIONS

1. What are manners?

2. Based on the story, name one way you can be kind to others.

3. What does Maevis share on the playground?

4. Who does Maevis sit with at lunch?

ABOUT THE AUTHOR

Vicky Bureau was born in Longueuil, Quebec, and was raised in South Florida. As a teacher, she developed a passion for the social and emotional growth of her students and later transitioned into the area of child and adolescent psychology after earning her master's degree in school counseling.

In addition to working with children, Vicky loves to be surrounded by animals and nature. She lives in Fort Lauderdale with her family: Billy, Khloe, M.J., and Max; her three cats, Alley, Baguette, and Salem; and her dog, Boomer.

Written by: Vicky Bureau
Illustrated by: Flavia Zuncheddu
Design by: Under the Oaks Media
Editor: Kim Thompson

Library of Congress PCN Data
Maevis Minds Her Manners / Vicky Bureau
Manners Matter to Maevis
ISBN 978-1-63897-458-1(hard cover)
ISBN 978-1-63897-573-1(paperback)
ISBN 978-1-63897-688-2(EPUB)
ISBN 978-1-63897-803-9(eBook)
Library of Congress Control Number: 2022932730

Printed in the United States of America.

Seahorse Publishing Company

www.seahorsepub.com

Published in the United States
Seahorse Publishing
PO Box 771325
Coral Springs, FL 33077